"All I've done is give you a book. Yo͏ lit learn what's inside it"
- Miss Frieda Joy Riley
Teacher, Big Creek High School, Coalwood

"All one can really leave one's children is what's inside their heads. Education in other words, and not earthly possessions is the ultimate legacy, the only thing that cannot be taken away"
- Dr Wernher Von Braun
Aerospace Engineer and Space Architect, NASA

"This little book really touched my heart. May all mums and dads read it and understand that their children can succeed and have brilliant lives if they are allowed to dream and are given the education and inspiration to follow their dreams"
- Homer Hickam
Author Rocket Boys/October Sky

"I never thought fatherhood could bring me so much joy"
- Sir Elton John
Dad, Artist and Rocket Man

"This book is a fantastic read. It's brought our family together"
- Karen Bingham
The Parklands Rocket Kid's Mum

"Art is what we call it when what we do might connect us"
- Seth Godin
Artist and Ruckusmaker

THANK YOU

This book is dedicated to all our rocket kids and my, your, their dads, mums and other creative carers - people who care for and about them. For all our futures.

We are particularly grateful to the staff and school community of St Saviour's C of E Primary in Paddington where our journey started after head teacher Ms Woodford said 'yes' nine years ago.

Also Parklands Primary, Leeds and their leader Mr Dyson who super charged that journey, creating many memories and friends for us.

It's not a box set. Don't read more than one story at a time. But do try to get into the habit of reading together every evening.

For time is the greatest gift anyone can give a child.

Macauley - The Parklands Rocket Kid

THE ROCKET KID STORIES

Self portraits of the children at Parklands Primary School in Leeds who drew pictures for this book. Sadly we couldn't fit in all the pictures, but are grateful to them all for doing such a great job.

THIS IS YOUR BOOK

Usually you shouldn't draw or write in books, especially when they're the school's, or a library's or any one else's.

But this is your book, so you can do what you want to do with it. If you're reading it, one story a day at a time with someone, why not start by drawing a picture of yourselves below now.

Your name:

You could photo/share with any other thoughts you have and things you do/draw when you're reading this book on Instagram, Twitter or Facebook tagged with #RocketKidStories @ST3AMCo We'll put some up at: www.steamco.org.uk/rkactivities

7

The Boy and the Trainset

(Draw your favourite toy below)

INTRODUCTION
THE GREATEST GIFT

This is a story, in fact this is a book, about the greatest gift.

A gift that might help you get a great job, which might help you make some money. Maybe lots. Maybe a little, or none.

A story about a gift that might bring you happiness.

One that might help connect you with other people where you live, in your country, maybe even somewhere else in the world because that's what happened to all the people this story is about.

It may help make you a few new friends.

Maybe all of these things.

It's a story about art.

It's a story about connections.

It's a story about how people connect with their art.

You with your art.

Because we say that 'art is what we call it when what we do might connect us to someone else'.

So, your art could be painting or photography, cooking or coding, dance or DJing, fashion or football, robots or rockets.

Art is whatever you do, that you are passionate about doing, that might connect you to other people, maybe people you do it with, or for.

We say 'might', because it might not, and it doesn't really matter if it doesn't, if you enjoyed and were inspired by doing it!

You might connect with people when they look at your

painting or photographs, eat your food, use your apps, wear your clothes, watch your play, marvel at your inventions or gasp as your creations fly though the sky.

Art is about a magical combination of three things:

- Creativity
- Technology
- People.

Creativity is the process of coming up with new ideas. They may be new solutions to old problems, old stories told in new ways or simply new ways of doing things.

Sometimes creativity can make some money; sometimes it might just make life and the world better.

Sometimes both. Whatever.

We often think of technology as being computers, smartphones and other high tech gadgets. But really technology is just a word for a tool that was invented after you were born. Babies being born today aren't impressed by smartphones are they?

So, before we had computers, the available technology included steam engines, and before that, horses. Maybe it was the hand tools that started with the flint stone axes and sticks that cave men used to chop wood and hunt for food in order to live.

There are red marks on cave walls in France that are thought to be over 40,000 years old. They are thought to be the world's first paintings, made on cave walls by the hands of cave men, possibly children on their parents' shoulders with only the light of a fire to help them see.

Yes, we can think of Art as the combination of creativity, technology and people.

Or we could just think of it as the paintings and sculptures that some lucky and hardworking artists got paid to create for people to see in art galleries around the country or even the world.

Or we can think of it as art for all, made by everybody for everybody.

This book was inspired by a story that started just a few years ago in Britain, in a county called Yorkshire, in a city called Leeds. This led to an adventure for a dad and a little Yorkshire lad and lots of other kids and adults since then.

The dad was called Nick who wrote this book and who had started running STEAM Co. Days in his sons' school in Paddington in London with other parents and other people who care for children and their futures. All our futures.

On these STEAM Co. Days, 'school days like no other', kids get to choose between twenty or so creative thinking and doing activities, many of them things that they don't usually get the chance to do at school or at home at weekends with their families.

STEAM stands for Science, Technology, Engineering, Art and Maths and we call these the STEAM Skills. But really it's all just about creativity.

All the activities on a STEAM Co. Day link back to the STEAM Skills and could include newspaper engineering, coding a BBC Micro:bit computer, learning to play the ukulele, improvised drama, making an electric car, making paper rockets, animation workshops and so on.

The activities are run by parents and other people from the school community as well as other artists working with teachers. They are great fun and very inspiring days for everyone involved.

When they go back to normal lessons, the children talk about them for the rest of the year. Quite often these activities helped them better understand what they were learning.

You could say that Nick's art was rockets, but it didn't used to be. Nick went to University to learn to be an engineer, but when he was there he learned to be a DJ. He used his engineering skills to make a DJ mixer so he could connect two record players together and blend one record into another.

Nick had never really thought about rockets until he went on a trip to New York. He'd been invited to a United Nations summit about the skills that children all over the world would need in the future.

While he was in America, Nick went to the World's Biggest Maker Fair, an exhibition of making and doing where he came across a couple of dads from California who had invented a brilliant system for firing homemade paper rockets hundreds of feet in the air. They gave Nick one to bring back to the UK.

Nick was asked to give a talk at the Royal Society of Arts in London, and halfway through, got his son to fire off a paper rocket into the audience. After that, they added making paper air rockets to the activities on STEAM Co. Days at his sons' school.

One day, Nick's 83-year-old dad gave him a copy of a book he'd found in an Oxfam charity bookshop which he said was the best book he'd ever read. It was called 'Rocket Boys' and is the true story of a boy who connects with his art and becomes very famous.

[Can you guess what his art was?]

The author of that book, Homer Hickam, gave Nick permission to share the story with schools in the UK and he started taking it to schools all over the country for half a day. Here he tells the Rocket Boys story in an all school assembly, teaches a class of children how to make paper air rockets and then launches a dynamite powered rocket in the school playground.

He called it the '#RocketKids' session and as you can probably imagine it was incredibly popular with boys and girls in the schools he visited. It was alos very popular with their teachers ,who loved it, and the parents and other carers in the school community who came in to see the rocket launch.

Nick has taken this session to schools from Cornwall to Carlisle and beyond, Scotland and Wales and connected with people all over the world. He even gave a talk by video link to Brazil recently, that was filmed at the Royal Society of Arts, where he had fired that rocket years before.

Rockets had certainly connected Nick, but that was only the beginning of the journey.

Art and creativity are the greatest gifts we all have. They are what make us human. Robots and computers will never have an imagination, be able to do art or connect as people do.

But the greatest gift for Nick was probably that copy of Rocket Boys that his dad had given him.

[Have you got an art? If so, what is it? If not, what could it be, what would you like it to be? How might it connect you]

An artist

(Draw more 'art things' in the space)

Macauley and his family outside parliament

(Can you draw Big Ben's tower in on the photo above?)

14

THE BOY AND THE TRAINSET
MACAULEY - THE PARKLANDS ROCKET KID

One day, Nick ran the Rocket Kids session at Parklands Primary School, a school on the big Seacroft estate in Leeds. This was like many places, where life was really hard for people who didn't have a job or much money and so couldn't afford to travel very far to see and do exciting things.

The school was the heart of the community for many people. They held a big Christmas Eve Eve party where Mr Dyson the head teacher invited everyone into the school for a Christmas dinner, to get presents from Santa and even see real reindeer.

The assembly part of the Rocket Kids session takes a whole school on a roller coaster ride, talking about art, STEAM Skills and rockets – not only the paper air rockets powered by STEAM skills, but Stephenson's Rocket locomotive, a train powered by the steam generated by a fire that boiled water in its boiler.

One day during the assembly at Parklands Primary and just after talking about Stephenson's Rocket, Nick noticed a little hand go up in the audience. The boy on the other end of the hand asked a question:

"Why haven't you told us about steam boats" he asked and proceeded to tell everyone about the most famous steam ship in the world, the RMS Titanic, that sank on its first trip, after hitting an iceberg on its maiden voyage from Southampton to New York City in 1912.

More than 1,500 people of the passengers and crew of around 2,224 died.

He also told Nick that the steel that the Titanic was made with came from a nearby Yorkshire city called Sheffield and how he had seen the story in the films Titanic 1 and 2.

Nick was really impressed by this little lad, who later that day made a great rocket. His name was Macauley, but we now call him the 'Parklands Rocket Kid'.

Two years later, Nick saw a short film, a television advertisement for the John Lewis department store, about a boy who had been given a piano for Christmas and how it changed his life.

It showed how by working hard, the boy not only learned to play the piano, but became a very famous pop music star and made millions of pounds.

The Sunday Times newspaper has a list of the richest people in Britain and said recently that the boy, now a man called Sir Elton John, is worth around £330 million. That's a third of a billion pounds! All from learning to play the piano and creating lovely music and heart-warming songs.

His art has certainly connected in more ways than one.

And his story certainly connected with Nick who made a copy of the film with words in subtitles that talked about creativity and the importance of art in schools which some people don't think is important.

He put the film on the internet and was delighted when it was shared by Elton John and in an hour had had over 50,000 views.

Nick was due to give a talk about the Rocket Kids sessions at a big conference in Cardiff the next day and called a school in the city to see they would like him to go in and do the Rocket Kids session.

They bit his hand off (which is a way of saying they were really really enthusiastic and keen!).

It was a wonderful session, and after the talk in the afternoon, and being just before Christmas, Nick had an idea and made a film to announce The Twelve Days of (Creative) Christmas Tour and that he was going to drive from Cornwall to Carlisle doing the Rocket Kids session in two schools a day.

He was loaned a super car by Peugeot, hitched up the Pop-Up STEAM Co. Day Drop Truck and hit the road.

In the assembly part of the session, Nick shows the children a film of himself when he was one with his dad and his first trainset.

Nick loved making things as a child, not least as he had little else to do because his family didn't have a television and the internet hadn't been invented.

His favourite activity was making a den out of a blanket, a step ladder and chairs as well as making models out of cardboard boxes, just like Caine's Arcade [Google his film].

Later at school he won a competion to program a computer game on an early computer but didn't do much more coding after.

He worked hard at school and was lucky enough to be the first person ever in his family go to University, where he learned to be an engineer.

So, you might say that the gift of that trainset was to Nick what the gift of a piano was to Sir Elton John.

As Nick was driving into Bradford on the Christmas Tour, he heard on the radio that a music teacher in the school he was visiting had been shortlisted for the Global Teacher Prize as one of the best teachers in the world, for which the prize was one million dollars!

It was clearly going to be a special day for the school, the city and creativity, so Nick made a quick call and was able to rent the biggest video screen he could find for just a few hundred pounds, when it usually costs a few thousand pounds to borrow.

It was set up in the school playground and Nick gave the Rocket Kids talk to thousands of people in the School Community there, which included people representing almost a hundred different nationalities.

You can see three photos of that on the back page of this book.

Later, when he was in Sheffield, Nick popped into John Lewis and told the manager how their Christmas advert with Elton John has inspired him and was delighted to be given a Lego Trainset, that had caught his eye.

A week later, on the Twelfth Day of the tour and after Nick had given the car back, the LNER train company gave STEAM Co. a ticket to Leeds where he saw the most wonderful production of High School Musical at Parklands Primary School.

Afterwards, Nick went into the office of the headmaster, Mr Dyson and when the Parklands Rocket Kid came in, gave him a present all nicely wrapped up.

Can you guess what was in it?

Yes. It was the Lego Trainset that John Lewis had given Nick.

A month later, LNER generously gave STEAM Co. two more tickets so that Macauley could go down to London, with his train set, where he spoke in Parliament at the launch event of the Art Connects 19 Festival of Creative Schools, Work and Lives.

Andrew Lloyd Webber, the world-famous composer and musical theatre impresario, gave STEAM Co. four tickets for his 'School of Rock' musical in London's West End not only for Macauley and his mum, but his dad and sister too, who had also come to London on the bus.

They had a wonderful time and even found time to go to London's world-famous Science Museum. Sadly, Stephenson's Rocket was to on loan to Newcastle's Discovery Museum, but they saw lots of other steam locomotives and boats.

Macauley learned a lot there.

Nick learned two things too. Firstly, that Macauley's dream was to be a train drive (freight not passengers) and that Macauley's mum was really glad Nick had given him the train set, as Macauley's dad had played with him a lot since.

What an amazing journey for Macauley. One that probably wouldn't have happened if he hadn't put his hand up that day and asked about steamboats, showing Nick he'd been listening carefully and understood what Nick was talking about but also that he knew things that Nick didn't.

He had shown how **interested** and **interesting** he was, the two things that people look for in someone else when deciding whether to give them a job opportunity, some work experience or even just to be a friend.

[Think of the last assembly you had, maybe one with a guest speaker and think of a question you might have asked them, so they'd think you are interested and interesting, like Macauley]

Macauley opens his present

(Draw your dream present in the space)

19

Homer Hickam and friends

(Draw your friends below)

WHAT WILL IT BE? PLAN A, B OR Z?
JUST PART OF HOMER HICKAM'S AMAZING TRUE STORY

Imagine it's 1957 in a small town called Coalwood in a state in America called West Virginia.

At that time, nearly everybody in Coalwood worked for one company in one place, and there's a clue in the name of the town that might help you guess what that job was.

Can you guess? Let's pause for a moment to think what it could be. Coalwood? Hmmm

The company that everyone worked for built houses for its employees and shops, where you couldn't really spend money. You had to spend special tokens that they paid you for working for them.

Have you guessed what the job was in Coalwood yet?

In the year 1900, Coalwood didn't exist. It was only built in 1905 after someone found something in the ground and dug a big, deep hole to get more of it. People came to live there and in just a few years over two thousand people lived in the town, nearly all of them working for the company.

Yes, Coalwood was a coal mining town and most people worked at the coal mine owned by the company. They dug a million tons of coal out of the ground every year.

Thank about that. What does a million tons of coal look like?

Dads worked there, their dads had worked there and grandsons were expected to work there simply because there weren't many other jobs in town and Coalwood was miles from anywhere else.

It's amazing how quickly things can change.

Less than a hundred years later, the company closed the coal mine. Today hardly anyone lives in Coalwood anymore. Even the school, whose students made the town world famous, is run down and derelict.

If you ever go to the town, on the road in you'll see a sign saying 'Coalwood', and underneath it another sign saying 'Home of the Rocket Boys'.

So, let's tell you a little bit about The Rocket Boys, who were a group of young friends, including a boy called Homer Hickam.

Homer's Dad was a boss at the coal mine and really hoped that Homer would work hard and do well at school and go on to University so he could become a Mining Engineer. Homer's dad had never been to university and wanted his son to do better than he had. He wanted him to get a really good job as he had to work really really hard underground for most of his life.

But Homer just didn't want to be a coal miner. He'd seen not only how hard his dad and the other men had to work, and while Homer wasn't afraid of hard work, he also saw how the microscopic coal dust in the underground tunnels in the coal mine dust had made his father dangerously ill. Other men got ill too, retired and stopped working altogether, but Homer's dad wouldn't stop.

It was as if the coal mine was his life.

No, Homer didn't want to be a coal miner.

He wanted a more exciting life.

Homer didn't have any sisters, just one older and sporty brother called Jim who was determined that he wasn't going to work in the coal mine.

Can you think why?

One of the most important things that a dad or a mum or anyone caring for children can do is help them think what they want to be when they grow up, or what to do when they leave school. And to help them follow that dream.

Many, many young people love playing sport and dream of playing for their favourite team and being paid lots of money. Or they might learn and love playing a musical instrument with the dream of being a famous pop star one day.

Many people do this and for that reason not everyone can. It might be because there aren't enough jobs for everyone, or things might change and unforeseen things can happen

For example anyone can easily break their leg, just by slipping while walking on ice. If you had a dream of playing professional football, your dreams would be over if you broke your leg and you'd have to think and find something else to do.

If you had not worked on other subjects because you only had a plan to be a footballer – your favourite plan, let's call it Plan A - you might have to go back to school to get your qualifications or get a poorly paid job that didn't need qualifications.

That's why it's always important to have a Plan B. Think of it a back up plan. 'B' for backup.

So, did you guess why Jim was so confident he wasn't going to work in the coal mine?

Well, he was good at football. Very good in fact, and his dream, or his Plan A, was to be a professional football player which meant he could go to University and play in their team and then play football professionally and make a good living.

His Plan B was to work in the coal mine, but only if he had to.

But he didn't have to, Jim made it as a professional football player and had a great career in the sports world.

The fact is that Homer didn't have a Plan A and didn't have any idea what he was going to do. He didn't even like to think he had a Plan B to go and work in the coal mine. It was more of a Plan Z, as it was the last thing he wanted to do.

Then one night he was out with his friends and saw a bright light in the night sky that gave him an idea. An idea to make something.

The first thing he made failed badly and nearly killed him. But his mum encouraged him to have another go.

So, he tried again, and this time he nearly knocked the coal mine down! His dad was very cross and told him to stop it and spend his time studying to go to university so he could come and work in the coal mine.

Homer didn't know what to do or who to ask, as he didn't want to work in the coal mine, so he asked one person, a person you can always speak to about any problems you might have in life

Who do you think that person was?

Yes, he asked his teacher Miss Riley, who gave him a book that told him what to do.

Homer tried and tried and tried again, and after a year or so, he succeeded.

Homer and his friends were famous for what they had achieved not only in their town, but eventually across the whole world.

What do you think they did?

Homer and his friends had learned to make rockets and made a rocket that went six miles high in the sky.

Homer went to University and then to work for NASA, The National Aeronautics and Space Administration who were responsible for America's space programme. Homer trained astronauts that worked on the space shuttle and the International Space Station.

After that, he wrote his story in a book called 'Rocket Boys' which was made into a film called 'October Sky'.

By being interested in rockets, by reading about how they worked, and by making them, Homer made a Plan A for himself, to work in the world of rockets.

His Plan B (or Plan Z) was never far behind.

But the interesting thing is that he ended up with a Plan C - a career as a successful author. He has written a number of successful books using his imagination and creative abilities to have great ideas for stories.

The lesson from Homer Hickam's story is to always be interested, work hard, keep your options open and be prepared to seize any opportunities that come along.

We've deliberately not told you the full Rocket Boys story here, as we didn't want to spoil it for you, as you really should read the book.

Whatever you do, don't watch the film first, before you read the book.

Why do you think you should read a book before you watch the film?

When you read a book you use your imagination and make it yours.

Also, we'd love to come to your school with our 'Rocket Kids' Session, where we'll tell you the 'Rocket Boys' story, make and fire paper rockets with you that can go over a house and then launch a real dynamite rocket in your playground that will go up into the clouds.

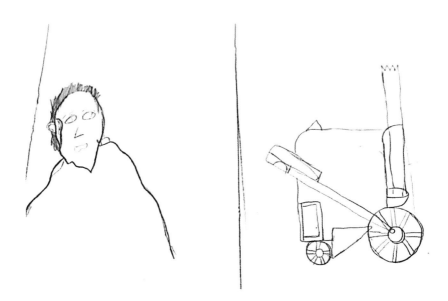

George Stephenson and 'Rocket'

(Can you draw Stephenson's Rocket below? Google it)

THE ULTIMATE STEAM SKILL
HOW GEORGE STEPHENSON CHANGED THE WORLD

In the early 1800's, life was very hard for many people, particularly in the coal mining communities in the South Wales' Valleys near Cardiff and the North East of England around Newcastle, Sunderland and Durham.

It was acceptable and normal for women and children as young as five to work for twelve-hour shifts in coal mines, some on the surface sorting and shovelling coal and stone. However many worked underground.

A law wasn't passed until 1842 to ban children under nine from working in mines and limiting the hours that children aged nine to eleven could work in a mine for.

To stop explosive gas spreading around the tunnels way underground, there were many gates called air doors which had to be kept shut.

The first job many children had in a mine was sitting by a door all day opening and closing it so that coal trucks pushed by women and children, or pulled by pit ponies, could get through.

There was no electric light, because they hadn't invented electricity, let alone light bulbs in those days.

The only light came from oil lamps and candles and only the lucky, better-off children could afford to have a candle to give them some light. So, many sat there in the darkness for twelve hours every day, opening and closing doors when they heard a truck coming.

It was dirty, boring and very dangerous work. Dangerous because as coal is dug out, gas leaks out of the rock and can explode. Guess what could light it? Yes, the candles. Another reason to sit in the dark to minimise the chance of being blown up.

George Stephenson was born in 1781 near Newcastle. His dad shovelled coal all day into the fire of a steam pumping engine to boil the water to make the steam that powered the engine to pump water out of a coal mine. It was a very poorly paid job, and because of that, he couldn't afford to send his son George to school, so, like his mum and dad, he was illiterate.

Do you know what illiterate means?

George Stephenson couldn't read or write.

Very few people today, especially children, can't read or write. If they can't, it might be because they had learning difficulties or had problems at school. But everybody in the United Kingdom can now go to school free of charge and not only learn to read and write, but study subjects that interest them to go on to a career or job they would like to do, maybe going to university .

Everybody has that chance, if they work hard enough and their parents and carers can give them some help along the way.

George Stephenson couldn't read or write and had a job like his dad, but working as brakesman, controlling when to start and stop the steam engine that wound the lift containing men and coal up and down the coalmine's shaft to and from the tunnels below.

George Stephenson couldn't read or write until he was 18 when had he saved up enough money to get some lessons and taught himself in his spare time.

Because of that, he could read the instruction manuals for the steam engines at the coal mine he worked at, so that when it broke down one day, he knew how to mend it.

He did such a good job that he was promoted to being in charge of mending all the steam engines. He became an expert and was inspired by the invention of a man who had come from Cornwall to Tyneside in the North East to share his ideas.

This man's name was Richard Trevithick, and it is said that he designed the first steam locomotive - a steam engine that could move on wheels. He went to Tyneside to build one for a mine owner there to pull coal more quickly and cheaply than horses could.

George was inspired and built his own steam locomotive called 'Blücher' – named after a Prussian general because of how quickly his army could march to support the Duke of Wellington at the Battle of Waterloo.

It was the first steam loco that ran on rails, with flanges on its wheels' edges to stop it coming off the rails.

It could pull 30 tons of coal up a hill at four miles an hour. As a guide, most people walk at three miles an hour, but not pulling 30 tons of coal! George went on to build many locomotives for use in coal mines.

In 1821, it was decided to build a railway line between the coal mines in Darlington and the River Tees in Stockton, where the coal could be loaded onto boats to be exported.

George Stephenson got the job of building the line and set up a factory with his son Robert to build the locomotives for it. The first was called 'Locomotion', and in 1825, pulled an 80-ton load of coal and flour at speeds of up to 24 miles per hour. It was the world's first passenger carrying railway.

In 1829, a railway was built and ran the 60 miles between Liverpool and Manchester and a competition was held to build the locomotives for it. George and Robert built the Rocket, which won the race and became the world's most famous (but not the first) steam locomotive.

For many years Stephenson's Rocket was kept at the Science Museum in London but moved to Newcastle for the Great Exhibition of the North in 2018 and to the Museum of Science and Industry in Manchester for 2019, from where it will go to the National Railway Museum in York.

Through all his work inventing steam locomotives and b uilding railways, George Stephenson became known as the 'Father of the Railways' across the world.

Along the way he made another important invention, a safety lamp that could burn oil underground without setting fire to the explosive gas. It was called the 'Geordie Lamp' and it is thought to be why people from Newcastle and Tyneside, near the River Tyne, are called 'Geordies' to this day.

But another man, a famous scientist called Humphrey Davey from Cornwall who was well known in London, had also invented a safety lamp.

Both Davey and Stephenson presented their lamp designs in a competition at the Royal Society in London, which was like a club or association for all the best scientists in the country.

Because he had taught himself, Stephenson wasn't considered an educated scientist and because he spoke with a Geordie accent, no one believed he could have come up with such a brilliant invention. They accused him of copying Davy's lamp and who they gave the £2,000 prize money to Davy.

Stephenson got nothing and was very annoyed.

He decided to make sure that his son Robert would be treated with respect so made sure he went to school and learned to speak without a Geordie accent.

Robert Stephenson followed in his father's footsteps, building locomotives, railways and bridges and became known as the 'greatest engineer of the 19th century'.

All because his own dad had worked hard and invested in the greatest STEAM Skill, reading.

Many people talk about the Three R's as the basics of education – Reading, wRiting and aRithmetic (which is another word for maths). What few people know is that there was a fourth 'R' for wRoughting which is another word for making as in wrought iron.

George and Robert Stephenson were certainly experts in all the Four R's!

Have they inspired you to make things? Maybe to be an engineer? The country needs lots of engineers and Hitachi Trains now build the high-speed trains that you can see on the LNER and GWR lines in Darlington, on a site very close to the birthplace of the world's first passenger railway.

The Tyne Bridge, Newcastle (and a great book about it and a dad)

Elton John in the John Lewis Film

(Scan this QR code to see

how it inspired our journey)

THE ROCKET MAN AND HIS DAD
ELTON JOHN'S SEARCH FOR LOVE

If your name was Reginald Kenneth Dwight and you had a dream to be a super star do you think you'd change your name?

And would you wear glasses to make you look like a famous superstar even if you didn't need to wear them?

And marry someone you didn't really love, so people would think you were like them, even if you thought you weren't?

Well that's exactly what Reginald Kenneth Dwight, a young lad from a council estate in Pinner, North London did.

He was a member of a band with a man called Elton and another called John and took their names as his own.

He liked a singer Buddy Holly, who wore thick rimmed glasses, so he got himself a pair.

And he did marry a woman, even though all the time he knew he didn't want to marry a woman.

Those are just a few snippets of one artist's amazing roller-coaster creative life that is as bright, diverse and colourful as a rainbow. It's a snippet of the life of the super-star musician and singer Elton John who is also known as Sir Elton Hercules John CBE after he was knighted by the Queen for his amazing charity work, particularly for AIDS and LGBT charities and the promotion of understanding and tolerance of difference.

His story is one of massive success and fortune as his wealth was valued in the Sunday Times Rich list at over £300 million.

It's also a story of hard work, creative talent, amazing luck and love. For many years though, he had a lack of love, despite having what felt like all the money in the world.

Elton's mum and dad didn't get on very well when he was young. They argued a lot, which upset him. His dad was in the Royal Air Force and was away from home a lot and was very cold and grumpy when he was at home. He didn't read with Elton. He didn't play with him.

His dad did play though. He played a trumpet in a band and without realising it, because he didn't make an effort to share his music with Elton, possibly gave him the greatest gift, a love of music by just playing a lot of music in the house on records and when he was practicing. Just being in a house full of music, of art, inspired Elton.

His grandmother lived in the house too and had a piano which Elton used to play, and a year later, his mum heard him playing a piece of classical music he had heard on the radio. She was amazed how good he was, without having sheets of music to read from. His grandmother arranged for him to have some lessons when he was seven.

Elton would play at family parties and other events, and at the age of 11 won a place at London's Royal Academy, one of the best places in the world to study and play classical music . This was on Saturdays at the end of a week at school.

But he didn't enjoy the classical style of music as much as pop and rock music, and at the age of 15, Elton got a job playing every weekend in a local pub where he loved to let rip like his Rock 'N' Roll heroes. These were the early days of recorded music, so every pub and even cinemas had a piano player to provide the music. He then formed a band and played with them and also with American artists who came to the UK.

The big break, and you may think it was lucky, came for Elton when he replied to an advertisement in the New Musical Express newspaper. It was for a record company that was looking for singers, song writers and band members.

He had an interview with the man who had placed the advertisement who quite liked Elton, but said he needed some songs and told him to go and find someone to write songs for him. He picked up a big pile of applications he had received from song writers and picked out an envelope at random and gave it to Elton.

On opening it, Elton liked the lyrics he saw which were by a man called Bernie Taupin, who he went on to work with for the rest of his career, to this day even.

For many years, Bernie would send Elton an envelope full of lyrics and Elton would write a song for each in half an hour or so. He was so fast; it was like a second sense to him. Elton would read words and hear the right song in his head and then write it down.

Here at STEAM Co. we particularly like two of their songs - One is 'Your Song' from the John Lewis Christmas advertisement because, as we have found, it really is a great song to promote art and creativity. Our other favourite is 'Rocket Man', which Mr Dyson, the Head Teacher at Parklands Primary in Leeds reminded us about two years ago when we first took our Rocket Kids session there, a school built on community, creativity and caring.

We have a saying at STEAM Co. that 'serendipity is our rocket fuel'.

Do you know what 'serendipity' means? If you ever read a word you don't understand, you should either look it up in a dictionary straight away or write it down to look up later.

Serendipity refers to events and happenings that seem to occur by chance, but that make you or other people happy, or good things happen.

So, it felt serendipitous to have been reintroduced to 'Rocket man' and the music made by a man like Elton John, who values art and cares and loves as much as he does, by a man like Mr Dyson, who does too, and who has won lots of awards for it, even though he isn't a millionaire yet!

Yes, Elton John and Mr Dyson both care.

In a symbol of his compassion and generosity, Elton launched a competition with YouTube to find someone to make a film to go with his 'Rocket Man' song. He awarded the prize money to Majid Adin, a refugee - who had had to escape Iran after the government persecuted him because of his writing and art.

He left his family behind in Iran to come to England by locking himself into a fridge, before being put in the back of a lorry for four hours.

In the animated film, Majid shows how he used his imagination to pretend that instead of fleeing across Europe to the UK, he was actually getting on a rocket to go to Mars. This was a wonderful demonstration of how powerful your mind and imagination can be to protect you from hard times.

Elton went on to have a fantastic career, making lots of great records that made people over the world very happy. His art connected with people far and wide. But he was very sad himself and became quite ill, largely because he had felt unloved most of his life.

Even though he had lots of money, it didn't buy him the

happiness he wanted, and he developed addictions and eating disorders and very nearly died because he didn't look after himself very well and felt he had no one who loved him. He felt he had nothing to live for.

It was many years until Elton found his true love and married his husband David Furnish in 2014, but it is felt that the biggest milestone for him was starting a family.

They now have two sons, Zachary (9) and Elijah (6) who both went to watch Elton John's football team in the FA Cup recently with David, while Elton played a concert in Italy. A dad's work is never done, and neither is a mum's, or that of anyone who cares about children.

Like many people, having and caring for children changed Elton's life, maybe as much as that piano had.

We often find this when people help us run STEAM Co. Days – whether or not they have or had or aren't going to have their own children. It's almost as if some people don't care about children or schools until they have children or work with them and then realise how wonderful it is.

In an interview Elton gave to the Daily Mirror newspaper in 2018, he said, "I never thought that fatherhood could bring me so much joy".

He went on to say "I've learned that the simplest things in life, like having a minute with them, are worth more than any painting, any photograph, any house or hit record. Before we had the children we just had our lives and we would spend money because we didn't have anything else to focus on".

It just goes to show that you can have nearly all the money you ever dreamed of, but money alone probably won't make you happy. Health and happiness aren't always that easy to find, and that it's the simple things in life, those we all have access to, that are often the most valuable and sometimes hardest to find.

As you have already read, Elton John's film with John Lewis has inspired STEAM Co. and made many connections, but it is his great story, his great art and the great job he does as a dad that inspired us.

The way Elton cares and shares the pleasure of being a great dad has inspired this book, even though his own dad could have given him more encouragement and support.

We hope this book, and stories like this, will inspire dads, mums and other carers across the world to be their best for their children, to help and encourage them as much as they can.

Importantly we hope that Elton's story will inspire all our children to go on to be their best, to connect with their art whatever it is and work hard at it.

And it is just as important that they are great parents for their own children too, one day giving them the greatest gift, of art.

Like Elton's Dad did.

Elton John and Family
(Can you finish drawing Elton John on the right?)

Space X Rocket
(Why not look for some coloured plastic paper/sweet wrappers
and stick it on the picture to make it look like fire for the engines!)

Elon Musk as a Boy
(Why don't you colour his clothes in or
even stick some fabric pieces in)

40

THE NEVER-ENDING LEARNING PIT
WHY ELON MUSK'S GLASS IS NEVER HALF FULL

It's hard to believe a world without the internet, YouTube, games and even television but it really wasn't that long ago that they didn't exist. And because of that, people did other things to entertain and educate themselves.

Just fifty years ago, in the 1960's, a young lad was hungry and thirsty.

It didn't help that he didn't have a television or the internet because he hungered and thirsted after knowledge and information.

This little boy's name was not Elton, but Elon, and Elon loved reading. He read a book every day. He read nearly every book in the school library, all the story books, all the encyclopedias full of facts.

Elon also loved reading comics, which are a great thing to read as well as reading books, because you use and develop your imagination and therefore your creativity so much when you look at pictures in comics with short sentences leaving you to use your imagination.

Reading comics took Elon to another world. He was growing up in a country called South Africa which in those days had a system called Apartheid where people were judged on the colour of their skin. It really wasn't a very nice place to be.

Elon dreamed of going to Mars one day, but first he had to escape South Africa.

He knew that he had a relative living in America, and he saved up enough money for a one-way ticket, because he had no intention of ever returning to to live in South Africa.

In America, he discovered and learned coding and worked on some of the first computers.

He entered a competition to design and create a computer game, which in those days were played on screens with fuzzy green text and graphics. They had none of the high quality and realistic images and sound effects we have on games computers and smart phones today.

He won the competition and went on to apply his coding skills in many areas. He started a company creating telephone directories on the internet, and ultimately helped to build the PayPal online banking system.

Elon had a very special combination of skills. He was not only very good at coding and other technical things, but also understood business and how to make money. Most importantly, he was very creative and applied his creativity to both.

He was also very determined to succeed and never let a problem stand in his way.

In 2002, PayPal was sold to eBay for about a billion pounds and Elon's share was worth one hundred million pounds.

What on earth would you do if you suddenly had that much money?

Well Elon didn't spend it all on new trainers and sweets. He spent some of it here on earth and some on going into space. He started a space rocket company called Space X.

He was also very worried about global warming and the

possibility of an environmental disaster and the need for man to find other planets to live on. Planets like Mars.

The first thing he did with the money was to help solve the problem with global warming. One of the biggest problems for the environment, after cows, is burning fossil fuels like coal, oil and gas to make electricity. So he launched a company to put solar panels on the roofs of houses, and his company Solar City became one of the biggest solar-panel companies in America.

More than any other, one project demonstrates Elon's determination to succeed and his ability to change the world beyond recognition, and that is his work on electric cars.

Before this time, electric cars had a very bad reputation and image, and nobody really wanted to buy them for anything other than mobility scooters for helping disabled people get around . Oh, and the odd milk float!

Stop and think about what the problems might be with electric cars at this time and why people might not have been very interested in them.

Well the first, as with most products we want people to buy, was that they did not usually look very cool.

They were considered to be very slow. And simply weren't fast.

They relied on batteries which ran out, so they were not able to go very far before they needed to be charged up again. They didn't have a good range.

And the other thing is that people often just simply don't like new things and like to stay with what they've got. We call this conservative or traditionalist thinking.

Elon was faced with a massive challenge which is often thought of as a 'learning pit'.

Imagine you are standing on the side of a river where you have lived all your life. It's your past and you want to move on.

Imagine the riverbed is dry with no water in it. You have to climb down your side of the bank, go along the bottom of the riverbed and then climb up the riverbank on the other side to be in a fantastic new place, called your future.

That was the challenge facing Elon, but imagine, in the middle of the riverbed is a great big wall that he has to climb over. Yes, his challenge was extra hard, to bring lots of electric cars to the world. Electric cars that that people would want to buy and drive.

Despite this massive challenge Elon remained optimistic and positive.

Often in life there are two ways of looking at things. For example if a glass has water in it halfway to the top, is it half-empty or half-full?

Well, it really depends how you look at. Some people who only ever see problems may see the glass as half-empty, which is a negative way of looking at it - a negative mindset.

People like Elon will usually see the glass and think of it as being half-full, which is optimistic and called a positive mindset.

A test you can try on adults is to ask them how they are today. Many will reply "not bad". What you should say to them is "do you mean 'quite good', because it's the same thing, isn't it?".

Do you think people like Homer Hickham and Elon Musk, with the challenges they faced, got up every day feeling "not bad" or "quite good"? Most likely they felt "very good". In fact they were probably full of energy and all the beans they need to solve the problems that the day might have thrown at them.

We call this positive thinking and it needs a positive mindset.

As well as positive thinking, one of the best pieces of advice in life is that if you fail to plan, then, often without realising it, you are planning to fail. (Stop and think about that for a moment - it's a very clever sentence).

Yes, Elon needed a plan and he came up with a three-stage plan, or strategy, which at STEAM Co. we think of as his 'Famous, Familiar and For All' plan.

The biggest issue that Elon faced in the beginning was that he was only famous for coding PayPal and selling Solar Panels.

Would you give lots of your money to somebody for an electric car if they had never made one before? Especially if you just thought that electric cars were boring, didn't go very fast and couldn't go very far.

So, Elon decided to set out to make himself **famous** for making great electric cars.

He went out to find the best people in the world for designing cool cars and battery electric systems and launched the Tesla Roadster.

The Roadster looked like other sports cars, because it was designed by someone who had designed sports cars and it went as fast as most other sports cars so looked great and drove very very quickly. In fact, it could go from 0 to 60 miles per hour in under two seconds and had a top speed of over 250 miles per hour. That's fast.

But it was very expensive, costing over one hundred thousand pounds and he only made a few hundred. But because of the advertising and publicity that Elon created for the car, everybody heard about it and saw how fantastic it was and almost overnight he became famous as somebody who could make and deliver brilliant electric cars.

So far it was all going to plan.

Phase Two of the plan was to become **Familiar** and Elon launched the Model-S car, which looks like an executive car was about eighty thousand pounds and he sold many more.

This car had fantastic reviews in magazines and newspapers, with CNN Television saying it was the best car that had ever been built. Yes ever.

This was a man who a few years earlier had never built a car , yet he had suddenly built the best car ever.

So, Elon became even more famous for making great electric cars, but they were still expensive and therefore not for everybody.

The third stage of his plan was to launch the Model 3 that would be even cheaper, so even more people could buy them.

He was very clever when he did this, because he held a massive launch event which he filmed live on to the internet.

That day, he showed a small number of the cars and asked everybody who wanted one to reserve one and pay a one-thousand-dollar deposit to ensure that when the car was built, they would be one of the first people to have one.

It was the biggest product launch in history, with hundreds of thousands of cars being ordered, each with a deposit being paid. In the next few months, orders for 500,000 cars were placed, meaning that Elon Musk had half a billion dollars in the bank with which he could go and build a factory to build the cars. How clever.

Today, Elon Musk's Tesla company is the world's most famous electric car company and has a global network with charging points in cities and service stations almost everywhere.

Importantly, all the other major car manufacturers have now

started to design and make their own electric cars, all jump started and inspired by that little boy from South Africa.

The one who couldn't stop reading and learning.

Along the way, he faced massive challenges and nearly completely ran out of money several times but kept going. He believed in himself and was always positive.

He worked incredibly hard but found time most weeks to take a few days off and spend time with his kids, often camping.

Do you think he read with his kids and encouraged them to read too?

The Tesla Model X Elecric Car
(Why not colour it in and stick some
tinfoil on to make it look real?)

Dorothy Vaughan, Mary Jackson and Katherine Goble

(Why not draw an Apollo Rocket behind them that they helped get into space?)

MULTI COLOURED MATHS LESSONS
HOW MARY JACKSON WON SOME RESPECT

Hopefully you remember from an earlier story how Homer Hickam looked up into the night sky and saw a bright light.

Can you remember what it was?

Yes, it was Sputnik, the world's first satellite.

Why do you think it looked like a bright light in the dark sky?

Even though it was night on the part of the earth where Homer was, the sun was still shining over the horizon and the Sputnik was still being lit by the sun, it didn't have its own light shining out. Have a think about that for a moment.

Now, a Satellite is a big electrical device around the size of a big dustbin, with aerials that receive electrical signals through the air from earth and sends them back to earth.

How could that be used?

Well, satellite television companies for example create their programmes in studios on the earth that they send through space to a satellite which receives them and then sends them back to everybody on the earth who has a satellite dish.

These satellite dishes need to be able to see the satellite in space which is sending it - that's why you always see satellite dishes on the same sides of blocks of flats and rows of houses, because if it was on the other side of the building it would not be able to see and receive a signal from the satellite.

Satellite navigation systems or SatNavs in cars and on smart phones receive a signal from a special satellite called a GPS satellite, which stands for Global Positioning System which sends the smartphone or SatNav computer data that tells it where it is.

The smartphone, or SatNav system are both connected over the internet to another computer which has been told where it needs to go so it can work out how to get there and give directions.

You may have seen photographs of the earth taken from space. Those are taken from satellites which have cameras fixed to them which send photographs as photographic data back to earth

Some satellites stay in the same position over the earth and some go slowly around the earth.

The Sputnik satellite was launched by the Russians for one simple reason.

Can you imagine what it was?

Here's a clue: the Russians and Americans were arch enemies at that time.

So why do you think The Russians launched Sputnik?

Another clue, The Americans were very cross that the Russians had beaten them to launching a satellite into space. They were quite embarrassed too.

The Russians were very happy however, because it meant that they could spy on America and see what they were doing and if they were about to launch a missile attack against them. They were enemies in the middle of what was called a 'Cold War.

Even though there was no day to day fighting, tensions were high between the two countries and a war could break out at any time with big missiles being fired to blow the other country up.

The Russians then launched a rocket with a person on it which annoyed the Americans even more, so they decided that the next best thing that they could do would be to get to the moon first. They set about launching a rocket that could literally put a man on the moon .

All this was called the 'Space Race'.

NASA, which stands for the National Aeronautics and Space Administration, is the organisation responsible for the American space programme and all their engineers and scientists were set to work to build a rocket that could go to the moon.

As well as engineering and science, space programmes like this require lots and lots of maths, for example, to work out how much fuel they would need, what angle the rocket would have to take off from, when it would have to be launched to make sure that it got to the moon just at the right time and so on.

Computers and calculators hadn't been invented yet and all the sums had to be done by hand by humans.

In 1961, Katherine Goble worked as a 'human computer' as part of the NASA space programme and she did lots of sums. Over and over again.

Because she was a woman, she worked in a particular area and because she was black, she was in yet another area again.

Mary Jackson worked with her and wanted to be a space engineer but there was only one college nearby that she could attend to study and they didn't accept black students.

They had one more colleague and friend, Dorothy Vaughan who was also black and acted as their boss, because black people weren't officially allowed to be managers.

It's hard to imagine today isn't it that the job you do, where you do it and who you are friends with depends on your sex and the colour of your skin.

What was even worse was that the only toilets they were allowed to use were on the other side of the site that they worked on and it was a long walk. This meant they weren't able to do as much work as they wanted to do, which was a real problem. This was because the maths that they had to do took a lot of time to work out and was very very important, yet needed to be done in a hurry.

One day, the boss of the project wondered why they were not in the office doing the sums as quickly as he needed them to and realised that they were taking lots of time getting to and from the toilet.

He grabbed a big heavy sledge hammer and smashed the sign off the wall by the toilet that said it was for white people only, a powerful step forward towards people being judged for the person that they are and not by their sex or the colour of their skin.

These three women went on to play a major part in the project and won many awards and medals for their work and finally had justice after being undervalued and treated very badly for many years.

This wonderful and exciting story is told in the fantastic film called 'Hidden Figures' that you really should watch if you can, so we won't tell you what happens!

But we will tell you to aim high and reach for the stars.

Whether you are a boy or a girl and whatever the colour of your skin, it really doesn't matter. In fact there are sometimes better opportunities in Science, Technology, Engineering and Maths based jobs for girls and girls from ethnic backgrounds.

So, what are you waiting for?

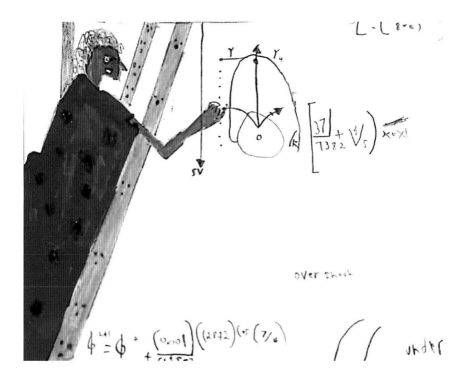

Scene from Hidden Figures
(She knows what she's doing, but why don't you write the most crazy and complicated mathematical formulas you can think of in the space below?)

Dr Helen Sharman
(Why don't you write a job advert for someone to go to space below? Think of the sort of person you'd want to hire and what they'd need to tell you to convince you to give you the job to fly your rocket! What skills would you look for?)

THE OUT OF HIS WORLD JOB ADVERT
HOW HELEN SHARMAN WENT WHERE NO MAN HAD

Do you think there is a spelling mistake in the title of this story?

If so, what do you think it could be?

Well there isn't!

We have deliberately written 'his' and not 'this' because, as you can see from the story above about those three women, many jobs in science, technology and engineering were considered jobs for men only.

But no more and this is a story about a job that is both out of this world and out of his world, because a man didn't get the job!

Many people think that the first British person in space was a man, Tim Peake, but it wasn't

The first British person in space was a woman.

Back in 1989, Helen Sharman heard an advertisement on the radio looking for someone to be an astronaut and to go to space. It said that no experience was necessary!

It was a project that was to be funded by a group of companies and a lottery. It was to be a collaboration, working with the Russian space agency as a sign that the cold war had ended and that we were all friends.

So, aged 27, Helen applied, along with 13,000 other people

who also wanted to go to space.

The winner was chosen as being someone who had a background in science as well as in education and aerospace. Importantly, they also needed to show they were prepared and able to learn a foreign language.

Helen won the place and then spent 18 months on an intensive training programme. In May 1991 she went into space and to the Russian space station where she carried out a number of experiments.

She has received many awards for this adventure and is now known as Dr Helen Sharman OBE. She does a lot of work to inspire young scientists and she now works at Imperial College, one of the world's top universities in London.

In an interview on the television during Norwich Science Week when STEAM Co. were in the city, Helen said there were three big things for her about going to space.

Firstly, the view from the space craft of the stars and earth which she said were magical. It really sounds fantastic doesn't it?

Secondly, she said she loved the friendship and teamwork, or camaraderie, of being in a team of five people on the spaceship. It's always all about people.

Finally, she said what amazed her were the things you see in space and how science almost appears to work differently where there is no gravity pulling things down. For example, she said that helmets need to have fans in them to circulate the air otherwise you would literally suffocate in your own breath as the oxygen is removed from the air near your nose and mouth when you breath it out.

She was also fascinated by the way that plant roots don't grow down like they do on earth but grow all over the place.

When asked what her advice to Tim Peake was when he followed her into space over twenty years later in 2015, she said to remember to look out of the window at the view.

Many people think you can see the great wall of China from Space but it's not actually true. But you can see some man-made objects on the earth like big cities and dams.

So far, 59 women have been to space, and as we said in the previous story, you really should reach for the stars.

So whether you are a boy or a girl and whatever the colour of your skin, it really doesn't matter. In fact there are sometimes better opportunities in Science, Technology , Engineering and Maths based jobs for girls and girls from ethnic backgrounds.

So, what are you waiting for?

Be sure to check out the great work of organisations like Dauntless Daughters, the Stemettes, The Royal Academy of Engineering, the British Science Association and The Institution of Engineering and Technology who all have plenty of information on great jobs both here on earth and up there in space.

Helen Sharman's view from space

(Why not draw all the other things she can't see through the window around it?)

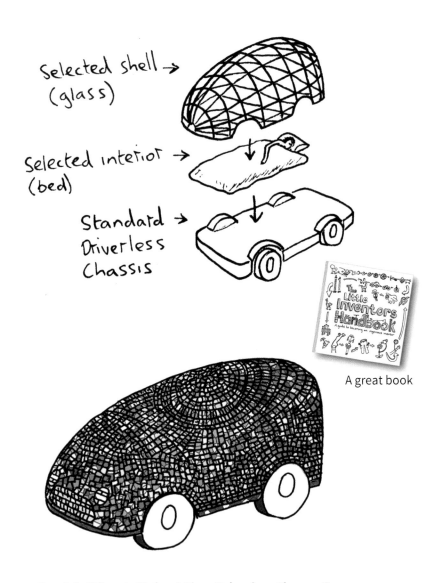

Selected shell → (glass)

Selected interior → (bed)

Standard → Driverless Chassis

A great book

Dominic Wilcox's Stained Glass Driverless Sleeper Car
(These are early drawings, see if you can find a photo of the real thing on the internet)

CATCHING DREAMS AND ASTEROIDS
DOMINIC WILCOX AND THE LITTLE INVENTORS

You'll hopefully remember what a 'Geordie' is, who is called that and why.

This story is quite crazy (or do we mean zany?) so to try to help it make some sense we'll remind you that 'Geordie' is a nickname for someone from Newcastle, a city in the Great North East of Great Britain that was once famous for mining coal and exporting it across the world.

That was done by boats which sailed down the river Tyne and out to sea, so it probably isn't surprising that there was once a thriving industry building ships in the area.

A city very near Newcastle called Sunderland became famous for building ships or making them and the people from that part of the world became known as 'Mackems' because they make 'em and (depending on who you talk to and believe) someone else would takem, either sailors who took them off to sea or Geordies who took them to fit engines in.

Whatever is true, all that matters here is that Sunderland was famous for making boats and other things. It was famous for its stained glass that was used in churches and cathedrals all over the country.

Mackems also came up with all sorts of great ideas and inventions, for example Sir Joseph Swan was a physicist, chemist and inventor who invented the electric light bulb that was first used at the world famous Savoy Theatre in The Strand

London.

This story is about making things, inventing things and using your imagination and creativity to the max. It's also about keeping your eyes open and looking for inspiration everywhere and anywhere.

It's about a boy called Dominic who grew up in Sunderland and a girl called Opal who grew up, in fact who is still growing up, in Canada. Opal is a 12 year old school girl and Dominic is a grown up man who is now a world famous inventor.

When Dominic was at school his teacher gave him a book of inventions and whacky ideas. Dominic loved that book and it inspired him to come up with his own ideas and inventions. All he needed was a pencil, some paper, his imagination and a brief – a problem written down that needed solving

Dominic's mum and dad took him to all sorts of exciting places when he was young. One day they took him to Durham Cathedral where he marvelled at the beautiful stained-glass windows. The round Rose windows particularly caught his eye.

(Funnily enough another local artist called Mick Stephenson made a light sculpture of the Rose window using coloured plastic lemonade bottles – be sure to Google it after you have read this story)

A few years later Dominic was at the world-famous Royal College of Art in London studying for an art degree and he saw a competition he wanted to enter. It was by the Mini car company, to design a car of the future.

Dominic sat down to think of ideas, ideas that were creative and different, ideas that no one else had thought of, ideas that people wouldn't just like but would love, ideas that would maybe even make them smile.

He thought back to his trip to Durham Cathedral and its stained-glass windows and designed the stained glass driverless sleeper car.

This was a car with a bed in it. Because it was a driverless car and could drive itself, you could sleep in it.

Because it was driverless, you didn't need to see where you were going and would want to look at something beautiful too, so he made the whole body and windows as one bubble of stained glass – all different colours.

It was beautiful.

As a result of that invention and many others, like the portable bottom seat and the teacup with inbuilt cooling fan, Dominic became quite famous.

STEAM Co. met Dominic at a STEAM Co. Day they ran at the top of the BT Tower to launch BT's National Inventors day in 2014. They invited him along to speak and run activities for children at their first event in Liverpool and later at Wellington College.

They also ran a big STEAM Co. regional launch event for his Inventors project in his home city of Sunderland> in the weeks before he'd run a project to inspire hundreds of local children to come up with their own inventions, several of which, like a high five machine, a family scooter and ladybird umbrella, he had made by local Mackems.

Some of these inventions are now in the world-famous Victoria and Albert Museum in London where they will be preserved forever.

The children that worked with Dominic on STEAM Co. events loved his ideas and they wondered how every child in British schools could be inspired by his creativity and art.

They came up with the idea of Inspirators – famous creative people that STEAM Co. could make activity packs with that could be used on STEAM Co. Days alongside other activities like rocket making, coding, improv, ukulele, etc and that's what they did.

The night before the STEAM Co. Day, parents, teachers and other creative carers that were helping watched a video by Dominic explaining what the activity was about.

Then the next day on the STEAM Co. Day the children could watch a similar film and create their own inventions.

Dominic got really famous and was invited to go onto a very popular television show in America called the Late Show with Stephen Colbert which was watched by about 2 million people every night.

Just before that STEAM Co. made up an advert in PowerPoint featuring Dominic and his Stained Glass Driverless Sleeper Car which they sent in to the British Government who used it as an official advert for Creativity is Great Britain.

As a result of all this Dominic became very famous and very popular and went on to create the Little Inventors project where any invention that was created anywhere in the world could be uploaded to his website.

Dominic and his team would have a look at the ideas and get some of them made up for real or in 3D so they looked real.

So what's this got to do with Opal, the girl in Canada we hear you ask?

Well the Little Inventors web site has lots of inventions in all sorts of categories including ideas for space.

Opal's invention was particularly ingenious and a possible solution to the problem faced by the international space station in generating electricity, which was done using solar panels that converted the rays of the sun to electricity.

The Band 101 was Opal's eco-friendly solution to this problem. It used a net in space made out of stretchy wires that conduct energy with a hole in the middle of the net.

When an asteroid hits the net, it will try to go through the hole. When it succeeds, the band will lash back and the bounce creates energy that will be sent back to the space station.

The idea was brought to life by local maker Chloe Rodham as a model in a film that you can see on the Little Inventors website by searching for Band 101.

It all goes to show that everyone can be creative and have great ideas but like any muscle, your brain, your creativity, needs to be exercised regularly to stay strong and get stronger.

When Dominic was a little boy he invented things every day, inspired by the book his teacher gave him.

Now you can be inspired not only by his ideas but by the hundreds of children's ideas that have been uploaded onto his website.

And maybe send in some of your own inventions from your wildest dreams. Who knows maybe he'll make up one of your ideas and bring it to life.

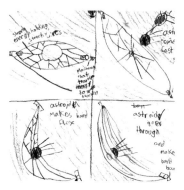

Opal's Band 101 Invention for Generating Electricity in Space

Yusaka Maezawa
(He loves art, so why not draw a beautiful picture behind him
or collage one with pictures from old magazines)

ART, CAN TAKE YOU ANYWHERE
YUSAKA MAEZAWA AND THE TICKET TO RIDE

In one of the first stories in this book, we talked about how the gift of a train set when he was one from his dad, had been to Nick what that piano was to Elton John in the John Lewis film.

In that film, Nick's dad shows him how to make a bridge by putting his arm over the track so the train can go under it. You can see a photo of this on the back page of this book.

Nick's dad had shown him how to use his imagination, how to be creative, how to develop and use his creativity.

You can think of creativity like a muscle. If you don't use it regularly it can become flabby and weak. If you do use it regularly, it becomes strong and so it is very important to always use our creativity to keep thinking, being curious and trying new things.

Sometimes it's good to be bored to push ourselves to find something to entertain ourselves or find new things to do.

A very clever man, Professor Guy Claxton, once said that "parents should allow their children to be bored because boredom is the engine of imagination".

An even cleverer person was Albert Einstein, who said that "logic can take us from A to B but imagination can take us anywhere" and this last story is about exactly that, a man whose art, creativity and imagination will literally take him to the moon one day.

No, we aren't talking about Elon Musk although the story does start with him

In an earlier story we talked about how Elon had been inspired by reading comics and books to try to go to Mars.

When he got his money from selling his shares in PayPal, he decided he wanted to build rockets.

Up to that point, the problem with space rockets was that they were only designed to be used once and were destroyed after take-off and old bits were left floating in space.

So, Elon started his own rocket company called SpaceX and developed rockets that could go into space and come back to earth to land on robot landing pads in the sea to be filled up with rocket fuel and used again.

This saved a lot of valuable resources in terms of materials used to make rockets. It has saved millions and millions of dollars for each rocket launch, and as a result,   Elon Musk's SpaceX company now does a lot of work for NASA launching rockets into space with payloads such as satellites and other scientific equipment.

Elon launched a rocket into space recently with one of his Tesla cars in the nose cone and a dummy figure sitting in the driving seat with David Bowie's song 'Star man' playing on the radio.

Elon Musk is very keen to start a commercial service where humans, not dummies, can go to space and he recently announced the first trip to the moon and that all seats on the rocket had been bought by one person, an artist.

Yusaku Maezawa is a 44-year-old Japanese billionaire, businessperson and artist. He loves art and music and when he was at school in Japan, he started a band in which he played the drums.

He left school and moved to America for two years, where he started to collect records and CDs which he sold when he went back to Japan through a mail order company that he had set up.

The company got bigger and bigger and so did his band, and when the internet was invented, he started selling items on the internet, adding clothes to the items that people could buy.

His internet clothes company, called Zozo Town became very successful, and he started his own label of clothes called Zozo which were designed to fit customers precisely.

He even invented the ZozoSuit which is a black body stocking type suit with dots on it that you can use to measure yourself exactly using a special app on a smartphone .

At the same time, he started an arts organisation to promote young artists because he saw them as being very important to the future of art. He now holds two art shows every year in Japan.

In 2016 he was in the news because he spent over $50 million on a piece of art by his favourite artist called John-Michel Basquiat. A year later, he spent over $100 million on another piece of art by the same artist.

Yusaku is now a billionaire from his online business, and in 2018, he made an announcement with Elon Musk that he would be the first passenger to pay for a trip on a SpaceX rocket around the moon

And that not only was he going to go himself, but he paid for all the seats on the SpaceX Starship and has said he will take six or so artists with him as part of an art project that he has created which is called #dearmoon

No one knows how much Yusaku has paid for this trip of a

lifetime, but he is said to be worth $3 billion, and having spent over $100 million on a painting, it is sure to be that sort of amount.

There is probably no better example of how art and imagination can take you anywhere than this story for if Yusaku had not had such a passion and interest for music, both playing and collecting it, he would probably not have started his fashion business that made his fortune.

A passion for art and creativity can certainly provide many people with a job and a career, and while it won't always be easy, it should always be fulfilling, because you are doing something that you love.

It is important to remember that making money and a career is not the only reason to connect with and follow your art.

It might be enough for it to give you something to be passionate about, to enjoy doing in your spare time as a hobby and most importantly, something you can do to connect you with other people in your community.

Because, as we said at the start of this book, 'art is what we call it when what we do might connect us'.

So, whatever your art is whether it's painting or photography, fashion or football, dancing or DJ-ing, robots or rockets, you'll always have your art and the connections it helps you make.

And that's absolutely priceless.